# ABOUT THI
# SUCCESS GUIDE

This No Nonsense Success Guide, like each Success Guide, has been designed to live up to *both* parts of its name . . . to provide you with useful No Nonsense information *and* to increase your personal chances for Success!

Thinking about going into business for yourself on a *part-time* basis? Mail order is the ideal solution: You can start ANYTIME, ANYWHERE!

Thinking about going into business for yourself on a *full-time* basis? Mail order is where many of today's new entrepreneurs have found their fortunes!

Your chances of mail order success are as good as anyone's — so long as you have the knowledge you need to succeed! GETTING INTO THE MAIL ORDER BUSINESS is your step-by-step guide into the exciting and profitable world of mail order!

# THE NO NONSENSE LIBRARY

## NO NONSENSE SUCCESS GUIDES

Getting Into the Consulting Business
Getting Into the Mail Order Business
How to Own and Operate a Franchise
How to Run a Business Out of Your Home
How (and Where) to Get the Money to Get Started
The Self-Employment Test

## OTHER NO NONSENSE GUIDES

CAR GUIDES

CAREER GUIDES

COOKING GUIDES

FINANCIAL GUIDES

HEALTH GUIDES

LEGAL GUIDES

PARENTING GUIDES

PHOTOGRAPHY GUIDES

REAL ESTATE GUIDES

STUDY GUIDES

WINE GUIDES

# NO NONSENSE

## SUCCESS GUIDE

# GETTING INTO THE MAIL ORDER BUSINESS

## STEVE KAHN

LONGMEADOW PRESS

Getting Into The Mail Order Business

Cover design by Tom Fowler, Inc.

Composition by Tod Clonan Associates, Inc.

Published for Longmeadow Press, 201 High Ridge Road, Stamford, Connecticut 06904.

No Nonsense Success Guide is a trademark controlled by Longmeadow Press.

ISBN: 0-681-40128-1

Printed in the United States of America

9  8  7  6  5

# TABLE OF CONTENTS

# 1

# WHAT EXACTLY IS THE MAIL ORDER BUSINESS?

Do you remember the way you felt as a child when you received a birthday card from your favorite aunt, who lived 500 miles away? Not only did she take the time and trouble to send you a card — but when you opened it up an unexpected five-dollar bill fluttered out!

What you experienced that day was *the thrill of mail order!*

There are few good feelings which can beat the absolute joy of opening up an envelope . . . and finding money inside!

Ultimately, that is what the mail order business is all about — successfully convincing others to trust you to the point where they will send you their money through the mail.

In business, of course, it's not as easy as receiving an unexpected surprise from your favorite aunt.

At any age, the excitement of receiving money in the mail never diminishes.

The purpose of this book is to help you to achieve that excitement on a regular, profitable — and continually thrilling — basis.

## You Will Really Be in 3-Businesses-in-1

The mail order business is exactly that — consumers sending you their orders through the mail.

The mail order business is also much more than that.

It is really three separate but closely related businesses operating under the convenient and logical umbrella of "mail order."

The three categories which make up the mail order business are:

1. Direct Mail.
2. Catalogues.
3. Newspaper and magazine advertising.

## Direct Mail

Direct Mail — or DM, as it is frequently referred to — is perhaps the most familiar aspect of mail order.

An offer — most often, a carefully written letter plus some additional written and/or illustrated material — is delivered directly to a prospect through the mail.

It is typically mailed in a standard No. 10 business envelope — and the envelope usually has some interest-provoking language on its face — copy or a headline designed to encourage the receipient to open it upon arrival.

We will get into the importance of "the package" — that is, the form and content of what you are mailing — later. But it is obvious that a Direct Mail package must be designed to succeed in its primary purpose: *To get opened.* A direct mail offer which is not opened is one which will not be given the opportunity to succeed.

When people speak of the "mail order business," DM is what they often have in mind.

## Catalogues

Think of the Sears catalogue — and this category of mail order comes into focus.

Today, this rapidly-changing and explosively-expanding category has developed significantly beyond the classic Sears catalogue.

There are currently thousands of specialized catalogues designed to appeal to specific needs and interests. Whereas in Sears (and similar) catalogues you can buy anything from a washing machine to a pair of sneakers, the specialized catalogues have a much more narrow and targeted focus. There are catalogues for cooks, antique collectors and joggers — and most every other hobby and interest you can imagine. We will return to the increasingly important subject of specialty catalogues in Chapter 10.

Entrepreneurs beginning a mail order business do not usually start out with a catalogue — but a strong, growing, repeat mail order business often evolves into one which adds catalogues to its advertising arsenal.


## Newspaper and Magazine Advertising

The classified sections of publications could be considered the "delivery room" of the mail order business — because they give birth to new mail order enterprises virtually every day.

Newspapers and magazines know that their classified advertising sections are two-way "gold mines."

They are extremely profitable sections for the publications — and they are ideal testing grounds for mail order entrepreneurs.    Classified ads quickly help the mail order entrepreneur determine if his product is a "gold mine," a wash-out — or somewhere comfortably (and profitably) in-between.

A classified advertisement is often the new mail order entrepreneur's first direct connection with his prospective customers.

The art of writing an effective, response-producing classified ad — and the equally important art of placing it in the "right" publications (at the "right" time of year) — is a critical one, and one which will be discussed at considerable length.

## Will You Be in the Direct Marketing or Mail Order Business?

This book is clearly and completely designed to help you get into the mail order business.

By definition, you will also be in the *direct marketing* business.

Until about fifteen years ago, there was no real distinction between the two. They were synonymous: If you marketed directly to your prospective customers, you were in the mail order business. Mail order and direct marketing were one and the same.

Today, that is clearly not the case.

Mail order — as defined by our three categories — is still the most significant factor in the whole scheme of direct marketing — and, from all indications, will remain so into the foreseeable future.

But because of the so-called "new technologies" and new direct-response techniques which have recently become available to those in the business of marketing directly to consumers, a new and larger definition which includes these developments has been formed.

Thus, the new home shopping television networks are part of direct marketing.

The use of 800 telephone numbers (both to solicit and to receive orders) are part of direct marketing.

And advertiser-sponsored home videos and computers linked to mail order companies are part of direct marketing.

These are all new, sophisticated and still-emerging — and often expensive and unproven — techniques for reaching the consumer directly.

As a start-up mail order businessperson, you will most likely not employ any of these available techniques and technologies in the early phases of your mail order business.

You will — as did Mr. Sears and Mr. Roebuck — put your trust into the hands of the United States Post Office.

There may come a time — and we will help you to prepare for it — when you will have the occasion and the opportunity to use one or more of these methods to support your basic mail order operation.

As a mail order entrepreneur, you are also a direct marketing entrepreneur.

No matter what you call yourself, your favorite six-word phrase will become: "The check is in the mail!"

*Best of all, it will be mail addressed to you!*

# 2

# WHY MAIL ORDER IS THE IDEAL PART-TIME BUSINESS

Ask a successful mail order entrepreneur to reminisce about the early days of his business and the chances are that he will tell you a story similar to this one:

*"We started small, right at home. We'd sit around the kitchen table opening the mail and counting the money (which was the best part)... then we'd put the orders together and send them out — often on the same day we got 'em.*

*"In a way — even though the business has grown beyond our wildest dreams — those were the best days of all!"*

The mail order business *is* the ideal part-time business because it can be started anywhere — in an apartment, in a house, on a boat! And it can be started anytime — today, tomorrow, the next time you feel restless and eager to do "something!"

*Anytime, anywhere* — can you imagine a better time and place to begin a business?

The attractiveness of starting out as a part-time mail order entrepreneur gets better: *Once you've decided to get going, you have the power to determine exactly how many hours a day — or a week — you want to devote to your new business!*

That is why, for many, getting into the mail order business is the most comfortable and satisfying introduction into the exciting and challenging world of the self-employed.

## Does It Matter Where You Live?

Absolutely not. A mail order business can be operated from anywhere. Some of the greatest success stories in mail order bear post-marks from locations far removed from the traditional business centers.

There's a basic premise in real estate that the most important attribute of a property is, "Location, location, location!"

In mail order, just the opposite is true. The location of a mail order business is truly insignificant. A mail order business can be owned and operated from anywhere — *so long as there's a post office in town!*

## What About Support Services?

Other than having sufficient quantities of your product on hand, the only services which you will initially require are a reliable local printer and the post office.

Using a small town post office — where you know the postmaster by his first name and see him in the supermarket on weekends — is no disadvantage.

All post offices — whether it's New York, NY 10001 or Zenia, CA 95495 — operate under the same rates and regulations. But it's a little known fact that the postal authorities at headquarters in Washington, D.C. categorize post offices by the volume of mail which they send out and receive.

Therefore, it follows that a small-town post office (which hopes that, in time, you might become a significant customer) is going to be especially helpful and accommodating to the newest mail order business in town — maybe even the *only* mail order business in town!

Virtually every community these days has a printer — whether it's the weekly newspaper or a so-called "quick" printer.

A local printer, no matter how small, should be able to meet most of your printing needs, which (at least at the beginning) will be relatively simple. Should he be unable to print certain items (such as BREs — Business Reply Envelopes), they can be ordered elsewhere. Just be certain that you order your out-of-town items well in advance of your need for them.

As you grow, and your immediate vicinity does not have some of the services and suppliers which you need to expand, modern communications should help you bridge the gap easily. Overnight express delivery services, FAX (facsimile) machines attached to your telephone lines and even computer modems connected directly to key sources will allow you to live and work in Vermont or Montana while closely staying in touch with your suppliers in Boston or Chicago.

## Getting Into The Mail Order Business
## Will Add Excitement to Your "Regular" Job

Two of the nicest things about getting into the mail order business on a part-time basis are (1) that you can arrange matters so that your mail order venture will not interfere with your regular job, and (2) that you will quickly discover that you have added a genuinely new dimension of excitement and anticipation to your "regular" work day.

Obviously, running a classified ad and then opening your mail box to disappointment is not a terrific feeling. But, in fact, there probably will be responses to your start-up venture, and you will find the simple act of discovery to be energizing. Then, actually filling the orders and beginning the process of gathering "names," which are the heart of every mail order business, will bring you surprising levels of personal satisfaction.

You should have no problem structuring your time, setting aside specific hours to get the mail, process the orders and develop new business prospects. If you have a family or children to help out, your ability to manage your time will be even more effective.

All of this can be done with a "low profile," without affecting your performance on the job. While there's no reason to keep your new mail order business a secret, there is also no advantage to broadcasting it. Even if you are working at a peak performance level, news of your "moonlighting" enterprise may cause superiors to evaluate your performance with a jaundiced (or even jealous) eye. Our recommendation would be to maintain a low profile during the part-time, start-up phase.

Starting a part-time mail order business while keeping your job is a little bit like an elected official running for higher office — but without giving up his position. If he gets elected, terrific! If not, he still has a job. That's a fortunate, fail-safe position — and one which the part-time mail order entrepreneur can enjoy, as well.

## You Will Have Time to Evaluate Your Product

By maintaining the security of your full-time job, you will avoid much of the stress of beginning a new business.

Not only will this have a beneficial impact on your blood pressure, it will have an equally beneficial impact on your business.

Because you will have something few new business owners have — TIME!

Time to carefully evaluate your properties, your methods and (most importantly) your results.

Sometimes, decisions made in haste are less than perfect ones.

By eliminating the pressure of "making it" immediately — by having the security of a steady paycheck in hand — you will be able to make business decisions more carefully, more considerately and perhaps more courageously. In any event, your decision-making process will take place in a less rushed environment — and that is an advantage in itself.

## Even More Importantly, You Will Have Time to Evaluate Yourself

Not until you are "out there" — on the firing line — will you really know (for sure) whether or not being an entrepreneur is "right" for you.

Starting your path to self-employment with a part-time mail order business will help you to answer that question. You will be "out there" — running ads, finding product, filling orders — but you will also be "safe" — like the politician we spoke of earlier.

Thus, you will have the time to evaluate your most important asset — yourself.

You will be able to determine your feelings about the mail order business in particular and self-employment in general.

And you will be able to do so without having to make a total commitment of your time — or your money.

Whether you enter the mail order business on a part-time or a full-time basis, you *will* have to bring to it a total commitment of your mental energy and your determination to succeed.

If you are so determined, the balance of this book will give you the information which you will need to succeed.

# 3

# THE LEGAL ASPECTS OF STARTING A MAIL ORDER BUSINESS

The mail order entrepreneur will have to deal with all of the legal details which are required in any new business — plus certain specific requirements which are unique to the mail order business.

## Selecting Your Form of Business Organization

You have three choices of business organization. Each has its advantages and disadvantages.

**1. Sole proprietorship.** This is the least costly and least complicated way of starting a business. A sole proprietorship can be organized almost instantly, so long as you meet local regulations (which we'll discuss later in this chapter).

Among its disadvantages are that you have unlimited personal liability with respect to the financial and legal obligations of the business and that (as the name suggests) the business will be entirely dependent on your good health and your good ideas for its growth and survival.

Nevertheless, because of its simplicity and directness, it is probably the most popular method of organizing a new business by an individual entrepreneur.

**2. Partnership.** If you will be joined in the founding of your business by one or more co-entrepreneurs, then forming a partnership is a possible form of organization for your venture. Legal fees for creating a partnership are usually more costly than those for creating a sole proprietorship but less costly than those for creating a corporation.

Among the disadvantages of a partnership are that it can be difficult to get rid of a bad partner; each general partner is bound by the decisions (and financial obligations) of every other general partner; and the death, withdrawal or bankruptcy of a partner can endanger the survival of the entire business.

Among its advantages are the additional capital a partner (or partners) can provide and the old adage that "two heads are better than one."

**3. Corporation.** Organizing a corporation is the most complicated and most costly of the three options. The greatest advantage of the corporate form of business organization is that its shareholders (its owners) have limited liability for the obligations of the firm.

However, the on-going accounting, legal and tax-reporting obligations of a corporation are considerably more demanding (and expensive and time-consuming) than those of a sole proprietorship or partnership.

There is a category of corporation which combines the protective feature of the traditional corporation (limited liability to its shareholders) while permitting the income (and losses) of the business to flow to you individually as if the corporation were a partnership or sole proprietorship.

This category of corporation is called the subchapter S corporation. A "Sub-S" corporation, as it's typically called, must meet certain legal requirements as established by the Internal Revenue Service. Consult your attorney and accountant at the time you are organizing your business; they can advise you as to the possible benefits or disadvantages of this category or corporation as applied to your personal circumstances.

## Meeting Regulations

When beginning a business, you will have to be in compliance with all applicable state, local and Federal regulations.

These will include such diverse details as making certain that your business location is properly zoned for your enterprise; filing a fictitious name certificate with the proper authorities (typically the County Clerk) if you are conducting your business under a name other than your own; and acquiring the necessary tax and sales tax identification numbers and authorizations from your state's tax and revenue authorities.

The question of collecting and remitting sales taxes on interstate mail order sales is a particularly complicated one, and one which your attorney and accountant will have to become familiar with on your behalf.

An experienced local attorney, one who has other small businesses as clients, will be able to provide you with a useful checklist of the regulations which you will have to meet when you are in the process of organizing your business. There are more than you might have imagined but, despite their number, they are typically simple and inexpensive to fulfill.

# The USPS

The post office — formally known as the United States Postal Service (USPS) — is obviously a primary element of the mail order business. Therefore, you will have to become familiar with its rules and regulations. A later chapter is devoted to "You and The Post Office," but no section on the legal aspects of starting a mail order business would be complete without mentioning the post office.

From the perspective of the mail order entrepreneur, the USPS performs two essential functions:

(1) It delivers the mail — which is the lifeblood of the mail order business.

(2) It protects consumers against fraud through the mail — and is very effective in gaining convictions once it has targeted a fraudulent mail order business.

# The Federal Trade Commission

Together with the USPS, the Federal Trade Commission (FTC) is the Federal agency which deals most directly with the interstate mail order business. Virtually no mail order business confines its sales within a single state, but we've made the *interstate* distinction because the FTC does not have *intra*-state jurisdiction. As a practical matter, the FTC will have jurisdiction over your mail order business since your mail order business will most likely not be confined to a single state.

The most important FTC regulation which you must know — and apply — is the *Mail Order Rule*, which has been in effect since February 2, 1976.

Unless your original advertisement, catalogue or solicitation advised your customers of a specific shipping date (such as "allow four to six weeks for delivery"), *the FTC Mail Order Rule requires you to ship your merchandise within 30 days of your receipt of the order.*

If you are unable to do so, the FTC has developed a very specific and very strict series of notices which you must send to your customers by first class mail.

Therefore, you must become familiar with the FTC Mail Order Rule *before* you begin your mail order operations — because it will in large measure govern the way you conduct your mail order business. To give you a sense of the Rule and its impact and importance to your mail order business, we are reprinting some of the FTC's most common questions and answers about the Rule:

*Question:* What advice do you give someone who is planning to start a mail order business?

*FTC Answer:* The FTC suggests that you do the following:
- Learn the requirements of the Mail Order Rule.
- Familiarize yourself with state laws in areas where you plan to do business. For example, some states, such as Wisconsin, have additional mail order requirements that should be followed.
- Ask experienced mail order sellers for practical hints to help you avoid the pitfalls in mail order business.

*Question:* How important is it to set up a customer service procedure?

*FTC Answer:* An efficient customer service procedure is

beneficial to you and your customers. Customers often complain that they have been treated badly by the companies they have contacted. But the number of complaints should drop significantly if your customer service personnel communicate responsively with your customers when they have problems.

*Question:* We advertise several products but do not indicate a shipping date in our ads. When must we ship?

*FTC Answer:* If your solicitation does not state when you plan to ship the merchandise, the Rule requires you to ship it within 30 days after you receive a properly completed order (that is, when you have received payment and sufficient information to fill the order.)

*Question:* What are the penalties for violating the Rule?

*FTC Answer:* The FTC Act provides that a person, partnership, or corporation may be liable for civil penalties up to $10,000 per violation. In addition, the FTC can sue for consumer redress.

*Question:* What can industry members expect from the FTC in the future?

*FTC Answer:* Because the industry is steadily growing, an increased enforcement presence can be expected. This may mean actions for civil penalties against firms who fail to comply with the Rule. At the same time, the FTC is part of a government-wide effort to encourage industry members to effectively regulate themselves. The FTC is working to assist businesses as they undertake voluntary compliance with the Rule.

For a copy of the Rule and other information with respect to the FTC's jurisdiction over interstate mail order sales, you can write directly to the Commission: Pennsylvania Avenue at 6th Street NW, Washington, DC 20580.

# 4

# THE PRACTICAL ASPECTS OF STARTING A MAIL ORDER BUSINESS

Owning and operating a mail order business, like owning and operating any business, requires you to constantly make business judgments — those practical details which will carry your business through the daily routines which form the operating backbone of any enterprise, old or new.

## What Are You Going To Name Your Mail Order Business?

Mr. Sears and Mr. Roebuck did what many entrepreneurs do. They named their business after themselves. This is an obvious choice, but one which may not always be suitable for your purposes.

Two contemporary examples come to mind. When Roger Horchow created his upscale merchandise catalogue, he used his name but added a descriptive word which helped to capture the elegance and exclusivity of his product selection. He called it: *The Horchow Collection.* When a Wisconsin-based company started out as a business primarily directed to boat-owners, it devised a simple, suitable name: *Land's End.* As the business expanded well beyond its original market, the name continued to be effective because it was catchy and memorable.

There is nothing wrong with using your name if you believe it is an appropriate and comfortable designation for your business. However, the name of a mail order business is also an expression of its desired image. Therefore, you should take some time to create a name which will work at the beginning — and continue to work as you grow.

Don't be too cute or overly pretentious or too ambitious.

Name your business by using the same guidelines which you will apply to its operation: Be honest, efficient and direct.

If, after considering these elements, you still believe that Bill Brown, Inc. or Brown Publishing or Brown Enterprises is suitable (on the assumption, of course, that your name is Bill Brown), then by all means use your own name in the company name. It certainly didn't hurt Messrs. Sears and Roebuck!

## What Mailing Address Should You Use?

As a mail order entrepreneur, you are asking customers to trust you, to send you their money — without ever meeting you, without having the comfort of a store to walk into, without really knowing very much about you. That is asking a great deal.

Just as one of the objectives in naming a company is to

create a sense of comfort and believability, the address to which you are asking customers to entrust their money should also provide them with a sense of comfort.

Thus, your objective is to establish a *safe marketing environment* for your customers.

A "cold" post office box will not do that.

Adding a street address to a postal box designation will help to create such a trustworthy environment. A "real" address will give the customer a sense of security.

The most efficient way to do that is to rent a post office box in *the same ZIP Code* as your home or office address. If you do that, then the mail will be delivered to the address directly above the bottom line of the address, as in this example:

> The Brown Catalogue
> 55 Mapletree Avenue
> P.O. Box 9999
> Cos Cob, CT 06807

The presence of a street address will increase your volume of response and will provide your customers with the assurance that they are dealing with "real people" rather than with a cold and distant mail order "vacuum."

## Your Starting Capital

If you are beginning a part-time mail order business organized as a sole proprietorship, your capital needs will most likely be (a) modest, and (b) entirely provided by you. Starting a mail order business without debt — by using your own money which you can afford to invest and possibly lose — is the simplest way of funding your venture.

Loans, unless you have the personal assets to support them *and* are will to personally guarantee them, will most likely be difficult to secure at the outset.

If you know some investors who have confidence in you and your prospects, they may be a more productive source of start-up capital.

If your funding is more complicated — say, you have organized as a partnership and some of the start-up capital is going to be characterized as loans from the partners rather than equity — you will need legal counsel to formalize such an arrangement.

The purpose of this section is not to advise you where or how to acquire the money you will need to start your business; rather, it is simply a reminder that your capital should be securely in place before you begin operations.

## Opening A Bank Account

If you have a cordial, long-standing relationship with a local bank, it is probably the most useful and comfortable institution to use for your new business checking account.

Initially, you may not want or need any special services from the bank, but by informing them of your business and its prospects at the beginning, you will have established a relationship which may prove useful at a later date.

## Making Arrangements
## For Extending Credit To Your Customers

Most mail order businesses give their customers the option of paying by check or charging their purchase to one of the major credit cards.

The ability to charge a purchase on, say, VISA or Master-Card is another "positive" signal to your customers. It tells them — just as a street address does — that you are "real." It adds another dimension of comfort and "legitimacy" to the transaction.

The new mail order entrepreneur must be aware of two things in connection with making arrangements allowing their customers to charge.

1. *It will carry a price.* VISA, MasterCard, American Express and the other major cards charge businesses a percentage of the price of each transaction charged to their card. This fee can be negotiated (and often reduced after you've established a track record of increasing volume and complaint-free service) — but it is an expense which you have to be prepared to pay and have to include as one of your costs of doing business.

2. *The major charge cards may be reluctant to do business with a new mail order business.* Thus, you will have to convince them of your commitment to quality and service and of your determination to build a long-term business. With respect to the bank cards (VISA and MasterCard), this is an instance where a friendly banker can be extremely helpful on your behalf.

To offer VISA or MasterCard, you will have to make arrangements through your bank or any other local bank which issues either one or both cards. To offer American Express, call 1-800-555-1212 and ask for American Express' "Merchant Services" telephone number. If the 800 operator is unable to assist you, write or call the New York regional office: American Express, Merchant Services, 708 Third Avenue, New York, NY 10017, (212) 557-2460.

Giving your customers the ability to charge can be a significant advantage to your business, and the general recommendation (without knowing any of the specifics of your particular business) would be to make such arrangements as early as possible.

## Lining Up Suppliers

You will need a reliable printer as well as other suppliers to get your new mail order business going.

Local suppliers — such as your printer — may be willing to extend some credit to you. It will depend on your reputation and your ability to convince them of your good business sense.

More distant suppliers — such as mailing list brokers — will probably require payment in full up front. In these instances, you will not be so much concerned with receiving credit as you will be with receiving their prompt attention and good advice.

In either event, make certain that you have suppliers who will be ready to deliver their services when you need them. In the mail order business, reliable and responsible suppliers can often make the difference between success and failure.

## What Are You Going To Sell?

We have covered the most basic and practical aspects which you will have to consider as you begin your mail order business.

We have, however, not spoken about the most practical aspect of all: *What are you going to be selling through your new mail order business?*

This question is so important that it deserves an entire chapter of its own.

# HOW TO DECIDE WHAT TO SELL BY MAIL

What are you thinking of selling through the mail?

A product you've created — or one manufactured by others?

Are you thinking of selling original products — or copies of already-existing products?

Are you going to be selling a year-round product which knows no season — or a one-time "fad" which has the potential of rushing into the marketplace — and disappearing just as quickly?

Finding the right product or service to sell by mail can be as easy as waking up in the middle of the night with a great idea — or as difficult as searching the flea markets of the world for a product which doesn't exist.

The good news is that you are surrounded by MOPs — Mail Order Possibilities. The difficult part is coming up with the ones that will prove successful for you.

## First, Do Your Homework

See what's already out in the mail order marketplace. Save

all of the catalogues and direct mail offers which you receive at home or at work. Constantly read, clip and save the mail order columns of your favorite newspapers and magazines. (The best indicators, of course, are those ads which reappear issue after issue. *Remember: Mail order businesses do not repeat unsuccessful ads!*) Listen to radio offers and watch late-night television (especially basic cable network channels) to see what's being marketed.

"Doing your homework" will give you a current "feel" of the mail order marketplace so that you can gain a sense of what products and product categories seem to be working successfully.

## Self-Publishing

If you have some special expertise as well as the ability to write, then self-publishing may be the ideal mail order business for you. You've seen the ads for books written by authors promising you a variety of different "secrets" for improving the quality of your life.

Self-publishing need not be that dramatic, or even in book-length format.

If you have some terrific recipes or useful gardening tips or how-to hints that can save readers time and money, you may be an ideal candidate for self-publishing.

Self-publishing can begin as modestly as a newsletter-sized sheet or a small, stapled booklet. The quality of the information which you are providing is the key.

The advantages of self-publishing as a mail order business are considerable: You control the product, you can deliver it simply (even in a No. 10 business envelope if your publication is newsletter-sized), and it is "self-liquidating." That is, you can print in small quantities and only go back for a re-printing when your stock on hand is sold out.

If you have the skills for it, self-publishing is an attractive and economical possibility as a start-up mail order business.

## Trade Shows

For mail order entrepreneurs, trade shows represent a self-contained treasure hunt! At one time, in one place, the mail order business-person will have direct access to *thousands* of possible products.

Most of the major trade shows are held in major cities like New York and Chicago, but if you are serious about getting into the mail order business, it is probably worth your time and expense to visit at least one show of particular interest to you.

There are gift shows and variety shows and housewares shows and consumer electronics shows and toy shows . . . and on and on.

The availability of unusual products, the ability to speak with eager (and hopefully knowledgeable) salespeople, and the opportunity to negotiate possible marketing arrangements (including a mail order "exclusive," if at all possible) make trade shows exciting spawning grounds for mail order products.

Obviously, you will not be alone and the competition for new products between mail order companies can be fierce and even discouraging. Nevertheless, trade shows represent a source of opportunity for mail order entrepreneurs.

Your library may have a copy of the *Directory of Conventions*, a comprehensive annual directory and calendar of events including trade shows. If it does not, the Index on page 95 will tell you how to contact the publisher directly.

## Governments: Ours and Others

In the United States, the official product information source is the Department of Commerce. For foreign governments, it is typically the Commercial Attache in the Consulate. In both instances, these government agencies are prepared to help you to find products.

The U.S. Department of Commerce collects and distributes a great deal of information with regard to products which are available in the United States from foreign-based companies.

(The Commerce Department's primary function is to help American companies market their products overseas. That is not the topic of this chapter, but it is something for you to keep in mind for future reference if you ever develop mail order products which lend themselves to international sales.)

A telephone call to your nearest Department of Commerce office will provide you with a rundown of their current services, many of which are free and some of which have fees attached to them.

The Commercial Attaches at the Consulates of those foreign governments recognized by the U.S. are natural allies for the mail order entrepreneur.

They are current and familiar with the needs and desires of their country's manufacturers, and will be eager to put you in touch with those who want to license their products in the United States.

There is typically no cost involved and establishing a personal relationship with a responsive, creative Commercial Attache can be a valuable long-term asset for your new (or established) mail order business.

## Business Opportunity Columns

*The Wall Street Journal* and *The New York Times* are the most prominent publishers, but many newspapers run so-called "Business Opportunity" columns.

*The Journal* publishes each weekday, and there is at least one mail order marketing possibility advertised each day. The Sunday *Times,* which is available nationally, is a thick and bountiful "bulletin board" of mail order possibilities, as well. Closer to home, particularly if you live in a larger city, your local newspaper may publish a "Business Opportunities" column which, over time, could bring you dividends.

Business opportunity columns live up to their name — they really do offer mail order entrepreneurs opportunities for new business!

## Direct Manufacturer Inquiries

Suggesting that you approach manufacturers directly reminds us of the old story about the beautiful cheerleader who never had a date . . . because all of the boys were afraid to call her.

Some of the very largest manufacturers (including so-called "household names") often have products which lend themselves to mail order marketing. Like the cheerleader, you will have to approach them to "get a date." You will be surprised at the warm and positive reception you will receive from many of them.

A classic reference series — *Thomas' Register of Manufacturers* — (which should be available at most libraries with a business section) will provide you with some of the essential information you will need in advance of making an effective approach to these manufacturers.

## Answering The Questions
## We Asked At The Beginning Of This Chapter

**1. Should you sell a product you've created or one manufactured by others?**

This is a difficult question but, typically, it will be easier and more efficient to sell products produced by others.

The most obvious exception is self-publishing, and other exceptions might include certain items which need your personal touch or the touch of craftspeople you have close at hand and can supervise.

As a general rule — certainly at the beginning — you will probably be better off (in terms of both your investment and emotional levels) to market products produced by others.

**2. Should you sell original products — or copies of existing products?**

Original products have a great advantage, but the cost of "tooling up" or otherwise getting them produced may be onerous. If manufacture can be accomplished with relative ease and minimum expense — and your promotion of the product is strong — then an original product holds considerable promise.

Existing products also have a great advantage. Familiarity. There is, however, a risk that a "me-too" or "copycat" product will be regarded as a latecomer to the marketplace and, therefore, be perceived as second-best.

The even greater risk in copying (or "knocking off") an apparently successful product is (1) that it may not be as successful as it appears, or (2) the owner of that product has hidden manufacturing or marketing advantages of which you are not aware. Copying is a risky business at best and may be a legal infringement on another's property rights, at worst.

**3. Are you going to be selling a year-round product with repeat business prospects or a one-time, one-shot "fad?"**

Fads — which typically require intensive, expensive promotion — are more suited for large companies with "deep pockets."

Repeat business is the strength (and objective) of most every mail order business. If you can develop and build a steady, all-seasons product, you will have a head start towards long-term success.

## The Three Keys To Mail Order Product Selection

The 21st letter of the alphabet — U — leads us to what we consider to be the three keys to successful mail order product selection.

*Unique* — The more special the product, the better its prospects for success.

*Useful* — The more real (preferably demonstrable) benefits a product offers the consumer, the greater its chances for success.

*Unavailable* — By this we mean unavailable in traditional retail outlets. If your product can't be found in a neighborhood store or at the mall, you have an obvious advantage: The customer has to come to you!

These *three U's* are an easy-to-remember, easy-to-apply checklist.

If a product checks out in all three aspects, it certainly is worth looking at more carefully — and perhaps even testing in the marketplace.

There are, of course, many other considerations which could be examined in connection with product selection, a topic so fascinating and challenging that it could be the basis of an entire book.

We have touched upon the fundamentals which should set you in the right direction. Coupled with the three keys which we just described, they should provide you with a comfortable sense of the mail order product selection process.

The bottom line is that for a product to succeed it must be valid — valuable to consumers and valuable to you. Consumer value is derived from the quality of the product; your value is derived from the resulting high level of consumer satisfaction. The mail order business is no different from any other business: Satisfied customers will comprise the foundation of your success.

# 6

# IN MAIL ORDER, "THE OFFER" IS THE KEY TO SUCCESS

Think about any business transaction other than a mail order purchase.

For example, think about buying a television set.

First, your mind re-plays the television commercials you've seen for the set (or, at least, the brand).

Then, you take another look at the glossy, four-color ads you've read in your favorite magazines.

After that, you may check out a couple of dealers.

Finally, after you've settled on a model, you walk into a store to begin the negotiation game.

Perhaps, if the price is right, you'll end up buying that television set.

The interval between the day you bought the set and the day you first saw it advertised could have been days, weeks or even months.

The advertising for the set was designed to "condition" you, to give you a positive image of the television manufacturer and his products, to eventually prompt you to make the move you finally made: to carefully consider and then ultimately purchase the set.

Now, imagine if that same television set had been the object of a mail order ad:

## SPECIAL MAIL ORDER OFFER!

*DIRECTLY FROM THE MANUFACTURER TO YOU!*
*NO MIDDLEMAN! NO "HIDDEN" COSTS!*
*"THE NO-NONSENSE SUPER-COLOR SUPER TV"*
NATIONAL LIST PRICE: $599.00
YOUR DIRECT PRICE: ONLY $449.00
— PLUS —

If you call our "800" number TODAY and use a major credit card you will receive a free designer TV table:

A $129.00 value at no extra charge for taking advantage of this limited offer IMMEDIATELY!
ACT NOW — AND SAVE $279.00!!

The difference between general advertising and mail order advertising is THE OFFER: *A mail order ad always contains an offer.*

The mail order advertiser doesn't have the luxury of time; he has to know as soon as possible whether or not his advertising is successful. That is why, in the above ad, we emphasized those words calling for immediate action.

The offer is the direct marketing link between the mail order business and its prospective consumers.

When you're selling by mail (using our TV set as the example), you know that your prospect can't test the reception of the set or feel the grain of the cabinet.

He also can't negotiate with you.

Therefore, he has to believe that your offer is the best possible deal he can get!

As the mail order seller, it's your job (and challenge) to convince him that it is, in fact, an offer he can't refuse!

Thus, it readily becomes apparent that THE OFFER is the key to mail order success!

## The Five Primary Elements of The Offer

**1. Price:** Obviously, price is a primary consideration. It must be fair and attractive — but it need not always be the lowest available price if other aspects of the offer enhance the value of the product to justify the differential.

**2. Features:** You have to emphasize the product's unique benefits. If they can be expressed visually as well as in writing, all the better.

**3. Credit:** You have to make the purchase as easy and enticing as possible. Advantageous credit terms can make the difference between a sale and no-sale.

**4. Incentives:** The customer is buying by mail, actual sight unseen. What "reward" are you going to give him for taking that risk? In our hypothetical ad, for example, we added the TV table as the incentive.

**5. Guarantee:** Your offer must contain a strong, believable guarantee; it is the mail order buyer's "security blanket." Our favorite is the one offered by Land's End. GUARANTEED. PERIOD.

# 7

# HOW TO DECIDE WHERE TO SELL

In Chapter 1, we noted that the mail order business consists of three categories: (1) Direct mail. (2) Catalogues. (3) Newspaper and magazine advertising.

How does the owner of a mail order business know where to advertise his product?

## Direct Mail

If the product lends itself to strong, lengthy descriptive copy which can be enhanced by useful, supportive graphics, then direct mail is a good choice as the medium to employ to introduce the product.

Direct mail is an expansive, expressive medium which gives you a great deal of latitude to present your product.

The direct mail package can contain many elements (which we will be discussing shortly) and thus allows you to use an assortment of attention-getting techniques.

# Catalogues

Catalogues are not the typical choice of introductory medium for a start-up mail order business. However, if, for example, your mail order business is an expansion of a successful retail store (and, therefore, you have a large inventory of products in stock anyway), then a catalogue might be a perfectly sensible media selection for you.

Catalogues are frequently an evolutionary medium for a mail order business, symbolic of its growth and strength over a period of time. A catalogue requires a consistent selection of proven products to support it. Thus, it is rarely the opening advertising gambit for a new mail order business.

## Newspaper and Magazine Advertising

If the product can be described effectively in relatively few words — and there are newspapers and/or magazines directed to its "target" audience — then print is your most logical introductory medium.

It is usually fairly priced, able to be scheduled on relatively short notice, and a fast indicator of success — or failure.

## All of the Above

In time, you will most likely use all three categories in a mix which works for your business.

Our observations here simply deal with a new product in a new mail order business — to enable the new mail order business owner to make some early decisions within a traditional media/marketing framework.

# 8

# HOW TO SELL BY ADVERTISING IN NEWSPAPERS AND MAGAZINES

Newspapers and magazines are ideal testing grounds for mail order entrepreneurs.

One of the primary advantages of advertising in a newspaper is that you can get a very "quick read" on the marketing potential of your product. If you run an ad on Sunday, you will have a reliable indication of the success or failure of your ad within two weeks.

Magazines offer you the advantage of a "mass medium" (reaching millions of readers in some instances) while still allowing you to direct your advertising to a specific, targeted audience. If you're selling a new kind of golf ball, you know that you'll be reaching your primary prospects when you advertise in one of the leading golf magazines. (Paying for audiences larger than your specific market is considered "waste." If you select your magazines carefully, you will pay for very little "waste" — and hopefully create a greater magnitude of profit.)

## Classified Advertising

If classified advertising sections didn't exist, mail order owners would have to create them! They are that essential to the entire mail order business.

If that sounds like hyperbole or exaggeration, it really isn't. Classified ads have served as the virtually instant and almost always inexpensive entrance into the mail order marketplace for literally thousands of entrepreneurs.

Classified ads have limitations, of course, including their small size, "telephone book look" and inability (in most cases) to accept photographs or illustrations.

There are also differences between classified advertising sections in newspapers and magazines.

Some magazines permit illustrations and their classifieds are sometimes grouped together in reasonably attractive "shopping sections."

Newspaper classifieds are almost always copy only, in an area of the paper far removed from the front page.

Remarkably, even in the face of these limitations, classified ads are a very effective mail order medium.

## How To Make Classified Advertising Work For You

The key to a successful classified ad is the headline. In a crowded marketing environment, you are competing for the reader's attention — and a strong headline is your most effective device.

Since you will be paying for your ad by the word (which is how classified ads are usually billed), your copy will have to be as effective as your budget allows. If it will cost you a dollar a word and you don't want to spend more than $25, make sure that every word speaks — and pays — for itself!

The best primer for preparing effective classified advertising is to read the classified ad sections in the publications which you are planning to use. The ads which work (that is, return a profit to their advertisers) will be frequently repeated — and they can serve as the creative springboard for your own insertions.

## The "Two-Step" Classified Ad

Sometimes, the purpose of an ad isn't to sell something right then and there — but later. That sort of ad is typically considered a "two-step" ad.

The first step is simply to get the reader/prospective buyer interested in your product. That's most frequently done with an offer similar to these: *Free Booklet! Free Information! We'll Send You Details At No Cost!*

The second step is really the use of direct mail (the subject of our succeeding chapter). Once you have a "live" prospect who responded to your classified offer, then you immediately mail him a complete direct mail package in the hope that he will be converted from an "inquiry" into a "conversion."

A "two-step" ad's success is determined by the number of conversions generated by the original inquiries.

This can be a somewhat sophisticated and time-consuming process. Therefore, it may not always be a suitable technique for a new mail order entrepreneur. Additionally, because the cost of your ad isn't immediately returned, your economic exposure may not be greater than a traditional classified expenditure — but it certainly will be longer.

If your product is moderately expensive and requires extended explanation, then the "two-step" ad may be the right step for you.

## Display or Space Ads

These are the non-classified ads in a newspaper or magazine. They can be as dramatic as the four-color back cover of a major national magazine or as modest as one-twelfth of a page in black-and-white in a weekly shopper.

It will probably be some time before you "graduate" to this level of print advertising. When you do, gaining an effective "position" in the publication will be a critical element in establishing the success or failure of your advertisement. Some positions, like back or inside covers of magazines, have premium prices attached to them. Others, like being on a right-hand page (always a favorable position), will simply require effective negotiation.

## A Special Word
## About Weekends and Newspapers

Reading the "Sunday paper" is a national family tradition — and your favorite Sunday newspaper is probably strong evidence of that.

Your paper will probably have a weekend magazine like *Parade*, a full-color comics section and a whole gallery of advertising pre-prints (those sections filled with coupons), which are referred to as "free-standing inserts."

Again, it will probably be some time in the life of your

mail order business before you can consider advertising in this often-productive environment.

There is, however, one direct marketing opportunity which you might be able to use sooner than you imagine.

The weekend supplements — *Parade* and *USA Weekend* — have an advertising category called "remnant space," which literally lives up to its less-than-attractive name. If, for example, a national advertiser doesn't distribute his products in twenty of *Parade's* markets, it will give up its space in the editions of the magazine printed for those markets. The resulting "remnant space" will then be offered to others at bargain rates — and, for a mail order advertiser, these opportunities can often be uncommonly profitable.

For advertising rates and information: Parade Publications, Inc., 750 Third Avenue, New York, NY 10022, (212) 573-7000. USA Weekend, 535 Madison Avenue, New York, NY 10022, (212) 715-5300.

## The "Key"
## To Determining An Ad's Effectiveness

Every advertisement which you run has to have its own "key," its own code — so that you can determine its effectiveness.

The key is usually a number-and-letter combination, indicating both the publication and the date of the ad.

*NYT1212* might represent an ad run in *The New York Times* on December 12th.

*PS6* might represent an ad run in *Popular Science* magazine in the June issue.

If your ad is a display ad, then the key can simply be printed in the corner of a coupon, if you're using one.

Most often, however, you will be coding classified ads. You have several coding options available to you.

If you are using a post office box, you can simply add it to the number: *P.O. Box 9999 — PS6.*

If you are using a street address, you can create a code: *Suite PS6, 9999 Main Street, Etc.*

In either event, the easiest method may simply be to establish a "department" for each ad. *Department PS6* for the magazine example; *Department NYT 1212* for the newspaper example.

The specifics of the key which you devise aren't important; making certain to *key every ad every time* is. You will not be able to remain in the mail order business if you cannot determine which ads are working for you — and which aren't.

The key to your survival is "the key" — the all-important code which you must attach to each advertisement which you run.

Newspapers and magazines can be useful and profitable mail order marketplaces. There has always been a special magic about print; deployed effectively, that magic can rub off on even the newest mail order entrepreneur.

# 9

# HOW TO SELL BY DIRECT MAIL

Imagine that you have acquired the mail order marketing rights to a unique product for dentists. You decide to advertise the product in your hometown newspaper, which has a circulation of 50,000 readers. There are 65 practicing dentists in town. Even if all of them, for the purposes of this example, are subscribers, perhaps only 45 of them will read that particular day's paper. As an advertiser, you will have paid an advertising rate based on a circulation of 50,000 to reach a potential target market of 65 — of which only 45 were "in" on the day your message was published.

Now consider an alternative advertising scenario: You put together a currently accurate mailing list of the same 65 dentists. You prepare personalized letters to each of them, together with some attractive descriptive material on your product and mail it to them by first class mail in an envelope with this headline on the front: *INSIDE . . . ANNOUNCEMENT OF A NEW PRODUCT WHICH CAN INCREASE THE PROFITABILITY OF YOUR PRACTICE BY 50%!*

Which approach will bring you greater response — and greater profits?

The second scenario, of course!

That approach has a name — *direct mail* — which is simple and straightforward. Nothing else about direct mail as a mail order marketing technique is quite that simple.

## The Advantages of Direct Mail (DM)

Our example highlighted some of DM's advantages. You can select your target audience without "waste." You can direct your message to dentists or florists or even parents of children under the age of three. Thus, DM gives you the ability to be selective.

(Usually, that selectivity is derived from the sophisticated — and not inexpensive — selection of mailing lists, which are typically rented for one-time use by mail order advertisers. Mailing lists — and the importance of your ability to find a strong Mailing List Broker — will be covered in depth in Chapter 11.)

DM also gives you the opportunity to personalize your message. A secretary can easily personalize 65 letters to 65 dentists. For large mailings which require personalization, many printers have the creative computer capacity to personalize hundreds of thousands of letters — and more. The cost per letter has dropped dramatically — and tests show that personalized appeals increase response dramatically, as well.

DM also gives you the space to be as creative as you wish. You can create a postcard-sized device or a giant pull-out poster. You can use black-and-white and no illustrations, or spend the money for a full-color brochure filled with photographs and custom-designed renderings.

Perhaps, most importantly, DM allows you to go one-on-one with your prospective customer: When he receives your

DM package, he has two options. He can open it or he can dispose of it. If he throws it away unopened, your DM package (at least with respect to him) will have failed. If he opens it — and begins to read the contents — your DM package will have achieved its purpose: *To present your offer to a selected prospective customer in an environment where — at least for that moment — you have no competition.*

That magic moment is every DM advertiser's objective, and the basic drive propelling direct mail as one of the mail order entrepreneur's primary marketing techniques.

## The 5 Elements of The Direct Mail Package

To death and taxes, you can add the five elements of the DM package as a given. Whether a mail order advertiser is selling a magazine subscription or a compact disc player, the basic elements of his DM package always remain the same. They are:
1. The outside envelope.
2. The sales letter.
3. The sales brochure, sometimes called the circular.
4. The order form, sometimes called the response device.
5. The business reply envelope, or BRE.

### 1. The Outside Envelope

As we mentioned, if your prospect never opens your direct mail package, it must be regarded as a marketing failure. Thus, you can appreciate the importance of the outside envelope.

Most outside envelopes feature what is considered "teaser copy" — a combination of a headline and advertising copy with only one purpose: *To entice the recipient to open it!*

Typically, the most effective "teaser copy" successfully presents *the benefits* of the offer to the prospect. If the prospect is convinced that there's "something in it for him" if he takes the time and trouble to open the envelope, then the outer envelope will have accomplished its marketing mission.

Many mail order advertisers devote the greatest amount of their effort and budget to the outside envelope of their DM packages. Given the importance of the outside envelope as an element of the DM package, it is an understandable priority.

## 2. The Sales Letter

The sales letter is the "anchor" of the DM package. It must successfully capture the benefits and advantages of the product or service which you are offering.

As we mentioned, more and more DM sales letters are being personalized. Whether you personalize your letter or not, it should have a warm and comfortable look and feel to it. It is really an invitation to buy — and it should have an inviting appearance.

New mail order entrepreneurs are frequently surprised by the news that lengthy sales letters often work better than short ones. If your letter "hooks" the prospect at the beginning, he will not hesitate to read an entire 4 or 6-page sales letter. A successful sales letter gets the prospect involved.

### 3. The Sales Brochure

Hopefully, your prospect has opened the outside envelope and read your sales letter. Now, he's in a "show me" frame of mind.

Your brochure is designed to do precisely that, to present in as creative and effective form as possible all of the benefits of your product. Photographs, illustrations, graphs — you can include whatever it takes to most effectively — and visually — demonstrate the value of your product.

(Since, in all likelihood, you will not be engaging in "sweepstakes" promotions, we will not get into the specifics of such a project. But tests indicate that the more the prospects become involved — even physically involved, by having to move a YES or NO device or attaching a stamp — the greater the probability of a response. That's why magazine subscription sweepstakes are so successful!)

### 4. The Order Form

Here's where the prospect is encouraged to take direct action. This is where, in the language of the salesperson, you are "asking for the order."

The order form should be simple, easy to fill in, and contain the most advantageous payment options your business can afford. As we noted in Chapter 4, if at all possible, you should give your customers the option of charging their purchase to a major credit card.

Most importantly, it should *never* be called the "order form." Call it a *Certificate*, a *Reservation* or a *Voucher* — anything but an order form! It should look valuable — green ink and currency-like borders are often used to convey this image — and have sufficient space for the customer to fill in all the information clearly.

## 5. The Business Reply Envelope — BRE

Most DM packages contain a BRE. It's easy, it doesn't cost the consumer postage and it often has the postal computer bar pre-printed to expedite delivery to the mail order company.

The only "controversy" about return envelopes is that some DM advertisers strongly believe that a plain, pre-addressed envelope *without* free postage to the consumer is more effective than the BRE. Their theory is that by making the buyer put a stamp on the return envelope, you are confirming his commitment to the purchase of your product.

That, however, is a distinctly minority view — and BREs are the return envelope standard of the great majority of DM packages.

## Who Should Prepare and Produce Your DM Package?

Chapter 12 deals with the efficient and economic preparation and production of mail order advertising materials for all three categories: Direct mail, catalogues and newspapers and magazines.

There are tricks and techniques to every business, and the mail order business is no exception. Even if you are confident about your skills and you prepare everything "in house," it might not be a bad idea — at least for your initial DM campaign — to get some input from an established mail order advertising consultant to make certain that you are on track.

Think of those 65 dentists. Direct mail, when successfully targeted and executed, is a formidable asset in the mail order entrepreneur's marketing portfolio.

# 10

# HOW TO SELL
# BY CATALOGUES

To a traveling salesman, an airplane is nothing more than a jet-propelled skybus which transports him from city A to city B. He doesn't consider traveling by air either glamorous or exciting — and he doesn't much look forward to his next trip.

To a child, the prospect of an airplane ride is the promise of adventure. To him, that 747 is an '80's version of a magic carpet!

Why are we talking about airplanes and magic carpets at the beginning of a chapter about mail order catalogues?

Because, in fact, the most successful catalogues succeed in achieving a remarkable status: *They are so successfully crafted that they become regarded as the mail order equivalent of magic carpets!*

Their audiences don't regard them as carriers of merchandise — which would be the mail order equivalent of the traveling salesman's perception of the plane. Rather, their audiences actually look forward to receiving each new edition with the same sense of positive anticipation that that child feels upon being greeted by a friendly member of the crew.

It's no wonder that the select group of mail order catalogues which has achieved this remarkable status is setting the standards for *all* catalogues.

## The Mail Order Catalogue Evolution — and Revolution

As we've already suggested, today's most successful catalogues have succeeded in creating positive images, in breaking through the so-called "clutter" of advertising.

Early in this century, the few catalogues which were published were "full-line" catalogues like Sears, which sold everything from liniment to top hats. Today, there are still a few national "full-line" catalogues, most notably those produced by Sears and Penney's. But Sears also publishes nearly two dozen so-called "consumer specialty" catalogues, each of which concentrates its merchandising effort on a specific area.

Consumer specialty catalogues are the fastest-growing category of catalogues, and they are the ones most directly in touch with today's changing lifestyles.

My own family is representative of the positive impact of these specialty catalogues. My teenage son looks forward to each new edition of *The Sharper Image* catalog as much as he looks forward to each new edition of *Rolling Stone*. My wife (who, like the majority of today's women, works) eagerly anticipates each new edition of *The Horchow Collection* and *Trifles* and *Bloomingdales-By-Mail.* And I will admit that I will read an *L. L. Bean* catalogue as thoughtfully as I read *The Wall Street Journal* each morning.

The mail order catalogue evolution has become a full-fledged mail order revolution — which has added an exciting new dimension to the expanding spectrum of mail order opportunities.

## The Keys To A Successful Catalogue

We've noted that the key to a successful mail order advertisement in print is its headline. We've also noted that the key to a successful direct mail package is the excitement and involvement of the outer envelope.

The catalogue equivalent of these mail order keys to success is its cover.

A reader — your prospective mail order customer — will take no more than a few seconds to look at your catalogue cover.

In that instant, he has to perceive a sense of the catalogue's uniqueness and value.

There are many ways to achieve that impact, but no matter which technique is employed, you've got to "hook" that prospect in that opening instant.

The two additional keys which follow are (1) your market and (2) your merchandise.

We will discuss your market in the next chapter about the importance of mailing lists.

Your merchandise has to be perceived as well-made, fairly-priced and fully backed by the resources and commitment of your company.

The catalogue itself — by a skillful blending of words and pictures — has to sustain this good feeling. If you can achieve this image — and live up to it by filling orders promptly and resolving customer disputes with equal speed and courtesy — your catalogue may eventually enter that select circle of catalogues which are welcomed with open (and eager) arms!

## Should You Start A Mail Order Catalogue Of Your Own?

The easy answer is no — certainly not at the beginning of your career as a mail order entrepreneur.

Like any easy answer, however, there are exceptions.

If you are already in a retail business, a catalogue may be a reasonable and logical extension of your existing business.

If you have the resources to collect a selection of products designed for a specific market (say, dog owners) and it makes more sense to sell them collectively rather than individually, you may be a candidate for a mail order catalogue.

Typically, however, a catalogue is not established in the early stages of the business cycle of a mail order enterprise. As the enterprise develops an inventory of products — and becomes increasingly sophisticated in its marketing methods — the creation of a catalogue can reasonably become a serious business consideration.

However, because catalogues are such an integral and rapidly-developing component of the mail order business, every mail order entrepreneur should become familiar with the primary elements of this exciting and evolving aspect of the business.

Instead of ultimately disposing of the mail order catalogues which you receive as a consumer, we suggest that you set them aside as a reference library for possible future use.

The catalogue you save may eventually become the inspiration for a catalogue of your own!

# THE IMPORTANCE OF SELECTING THE RIGHT MAILING LISTS — AND MAILING LIST BROKERS

The best mail order and ad ever created would fail if it was directed to the wrong market!

Remember that thought — and you begin to understand the critical importance of mailing lists in the mail order business.

The importance of mailing lists cannot be over-stated.

They are the primary building block of *every* mail order business!

The ability to effectively select and use mailing lists is the key to the long-term success of a mail order business.

The failure to develop that skill will inevitably lead to the eventual failure of the mail order business itself.

## Why Are Mailing Lists So Critical?

The mail order business lives up to its name: It's a business where people order products and services by mail.

*Before they can find you, you have to find them — and that's what mailing lists are all about!*

They are the mail order entrepreneur's prospects, his marketplace, his source of revenue.

There are fundamentally three types of mailing lists:

## 1. Your Own List

Obviously, developing your own list takes time — and money. However, no list will ever be as profitable for you as your own list of customers.

Over time, as your business grows and your customer list becomes a formidable asset, you will be able to profitably use your own list time and again.

At the beginning, however, you will have to turn to others as a source of names — which is what mailing lists are.

## 2. Compiled Lists

Thousands of these lists are available, covering every imaginable aspect of society.

They have obvious value — simply because you don't have the time and resources to compile such a list yourself.

They also have the disadvantage of being so broad that each list will require careful evaluation to see it it will work for your particular product.

However, if you want to reach doctors or auto mechanics or schoolteachers — as general categories — compiled lists provide a fast and relatively inexpensive solution.

### 3. Other People's Customers

Next to your own proprietary list, these lists can be the most profitable and effective — because they consist of proven mail buyers. They may not necessarily buy from you, but they have bought — by mail — from someone.

These lists are the most expensive to rent.

## How Do You Find Suitable Mailing Lists?

A company called Standard Rate and Data Service (SRDS) publishes a directory called *Direct Mail List Rates & Data.* To paraphrase the title of a recently popular book, it will tell you "everything you ever wanted to know about mailing lists."

Your best bet is to get in touch with a mailing list broker — one who is willing to work with a new, start-up mail order business.

As a real estate broker sells houses, a mailing list broker sells lists.

He really doesn't sell them, however. Rather, he *rents* them. Mailing lists are not for sale, in the traditional sense. They are rented for *one-time use only.*

A knowledgeable mailing list broker who is willing to work with you can be the key to your success in the mail order business. He will have the ability to match your needs with lists that he believes will work for you. If he is correct in his judgments, you will have gained an immeasureable marketing advantage.

## How Do You Know If A Particular List Will Work For You?

There is only one way to establish the answer to this question — and it is the way every mail business determines the value of its lists: *By testing.*

"Test" is the most important four-letter word in the mail order entrepreneur's vocabulary!

*Reader's Digest wouldn't think of mailing millions of direct mail packages without testing . . . nor would Time-Life Books or the Columbia Record Club . . . or any mail order business which wants to stay in business!*

The mail order business has different parameters than traditional retail businesses.

If only 1% of the fans in the stands bought hot dogs from the vendor selling them, he would soon be in trouble.

If a mailing returns 1%, under many circumstances it is considered a winner. Under any circumstances, a 3% return is a home run!

With such close margins, you can understand why a list has to be tested before you make the investment of a larger mailing.

There are varying "rules" regarding the most useful size of a test. The one we prefer is quite simple: 30 to 50 positive responses can give you a useful sense of the success of a particular mailing. Therefore — using the probability of a 1% response — you will need to test between 3000 and 5000 names per list to determine its effectiveness.

## "RFM" — And Other Miscellaneous Details

RFM is a traditional way of measuring the probable usefulness of a mailing list.

The R represents "recency." How recently has the prospect ordered by mail? The more recently, the greater his potential value — because he is truly a "live" prospect.

The F represents "frequently." How often does he buy by mail? Again, the greater the frequency, the greater his potential value to you.

The M represents his "monetary" value. In other words, how much has he spent ordering by mail? Obviously, someone who spends $5 for a book is not necessarily a prime prospect for a $45 sweater.

There are other measuring formulas, but RFM is perhaps the most common.

A couple of additional mailing list basics: Typically, the mailing list owner will want to see what you will be mailing so that he can approve. His names are an asset and he does not want to reduce that asset by exposing it to what he considers inappropriate material. You will probably have the option to make certain specific selections, such as ZIP Codes. There is usually an extra "selection charge," but depending on your objectives, that can be a worthwhile expenditure.

## Eventually, You Will Be A List "Landlord" As Well As List Rentor

In time, your own mailing list will become a valuable asset. Even a relatively small list can produce impressive profits.

Say you have 10,000 names which you can rent for a rate of $70 per 1000. Thus, each rental of your complete list will gross $700. The typical list broker's commission is 20% — or, in this example, $140, leaving you with a net profit of

$560 per rental. If you rent your list twenty times per year (which is not an unreasonable figure), you would suddenly have an annual incremental income of $11,200 — without having to work any harder than you already do.

As your list grows, you may have to computerize it. You can do this yourself or give the project to a computer service bureau with mailing list expertise. There are many such organizations. However, if you have a computer or intend to acquire one, there is a great deal of software available which will help you to put your mailing list on tape with considerable efficiency, simplicity and economy.

Once on computer, you will be able to "purge" and "merge" your list. By "purging" duplicate names and "merging" unduplicated names into a "clean" and current list, you will achieve two benefits: You will save money on your own mailings and rentors will achieve better results from your list — encouraging very profitable repeat business.

For many mail order businesses, their list rental income is a significant component of their bottom line.

The selection and use of mailing lists *is* as important as we suggested at the beginning of this chapter. We have only touched upon some of the most fundamental basics.

In time, you will develop your own skills in this critical area. At the beginning, you would do well to find a mailing list expert to help you make your selections. His fee should be considered an investment as well as an ordinary business expense because if he is successful, you will be successful.

# HOW TO PRODUCE INEXPENSIVE YET EFFECTIVE MAIL ORDER ADVERTISING

To us, the most expensive word in the English language is "overhead."

The new mail order entrepreneur has to be careful to keep his overhead — his fixed expenses — as low as possible. There are many opportunities to keep close tabs on expenses.

However, very few of us can do everything.

Thus, even the most talented mail order businessperson will have to draw on the skills and abilities of others. This chapter does not deal with administrative or office personnel; this chapter is devoted to the acquisition of the creative help you will need as you launch your new business.

## Finding Writers

Writing mail order copy is a special skill. You have to have the ability to hold people's attention *and* the ability to convince them to make the decision to buy right then and there. It is not an easy task.

Even if you feel confident and comfortable about your writing skills, in the beginning — like a cautious physician — you should get a "second opinion."

Your family and friends don't qualify for this task.

You should find a mail order copy professional and arrange a reasonable fee for him to evaluate your material. You should be familiar with his portfolio and confident of his competence; if you are, you should be responsive to his suggestions and let him work with you. Sometimes, something as simple as changing a single word can make the difference in the success or failure of an advertisement.

If you are prepared to delegate the complete task of writing copy for your ad or direct mail package, then this same advertising professional might fill the bill, as well.

If you do choose to assign the writing to an outsider, make certain that he has considerable mail order skills and experience. An elegant magazine writer or successful newspaperperson might be extremely good at what he does — but the chances are that he won't be good for you!

The two major national weekly advertising newspapers always carry ads for free-lance mail order copywriters. They are *Advertising Age* and *Adweek*, and they are a wonderful resource of talent for the start-up mail order entrepreneur. *Advertising Age* publishes one national edition and can be ordered by calling 1-800-331-1700, Operator 289. *Adweek* publishes five regional editions and can be ordered by calling 1-800-824-7888, Operator 172.

Writers, like all of your creative free-lancers, can be paid fees as independent contractors. Therefore, you will not have to deduct taxes, pay Social Security, or get involved in any other administrative burdens with regard to their assignments.

## Finding Art Directors

You will observe that we didn't caption this section: *Finding Artists.*

Our choice of description was deliberate — because you don't require the services of an artist. You require the services of an art director with mail order experience — who knows what combination of type and color and illustrations will have the most favorable impact on the consumer.

Advertising agency employees willing to "moonlight" and advertising trade publications are your most productive source of talent.

Most importantly, you will want to hire someone willing to transmit your vision — your sense of what it will take to sell your product. He will have to be skillful enough to bring that vision to life, but he will have to be willing to work within the pragmatic constraints you set out.

You don't want an art director who wants to win awards. You want one who is as committed as you are to sell merchandise — so that he will be asked back next month to create another ad!

## Finding Illustrators

There are those who, in the completely understandable pursuit of wanting to save you money, will suggest that you use a "stock" photograph or "clip" art for your mail order advertising. Both forms of illustration are readily available and relatively inexpensive.

We respectfully disagree — although we are equally determined to save you money.

Consumers have good and strong instincts. If they sense an element of "cheapness" in your advertising, they will begin to worry about the quality of your product.

Keep your expenses down by carefully determining your graphic needs.

A single well-structured, professionally-done photograph will not carry a prohibitive cost — and it will set your advertising apart.

An illustration should be simple — leaving the details to the consumer's imagination. Often, an inexpensive line drawing can meet your marketing objective. It will not cost much — especially if you can find a graphic artist willing to "invest" his skills with you at reduced rates in anticipation of future assignments at his standard fee.

## Your Contribution To The Creative Process

If you are not doing any of the actual writing or layout, then you will be filling the function of Creative Director.

Hopefully, you know what you want — what the "look" and "feel" of your advertising should be.

If you've done your homework and have a confident sense of what elements are needed to create a successful mail order ad, make certain that the elements you want are included in the final product.

You *can* create successful mail order advertising inexpensively.

You don't need a permanent staff; you simply need a pool of good, honest, skillful, hard-working people willing to help you to get off on the right foot.

They *are* "out there" — and they are just as anxious to find you as you are to find them.

# 13

# HOW TO MAKE THE POST OFFICE WORK FOR YOU

You will need the postal service to get your orders.

You have no option in this regard: Everything you mail will have to be transmitted by the USPS — United States Postal Service. Delivering the mail is their business — and no one else's — and you will have to depend on the postal service to deliver your messages to your prospective consumers.

You do, however, have options when it comes to fulfilling your orders. Depending on the nature of your business, you may elect to use an alternative carrier such as UPS (United Parcel Service) to deliver your orders. Of course, the postal service is available for that purpose, as well.

In any event, as a mail order businessperson, you will have to become familiar with postal requirements so that you can make the most efficient and economical use of one of your primary links to your market.

## Introduce Yourself
## To Your Local Post Office

The post office is a business and, like any business with an eye to the future, it welcomes new customers. As a new mail order owner, you represent more than simply new business — you represent a potentially significant volume of new business.

As we noted in Chapter 2, your local postmaster or branch manager will usually be as helpful and informative as possible, acquainting you with the postal aspects you will need to know to operate your mail order business without unintentionally running afoul of a myriad of rules and regulations.

Establishing a productive relationship with his primary post office is an early priority for the new mail order businessperson.


## Using Third Class "Bulk Mail"

The minimum third class "bulk mail" rate covers the first two and a fraction ounces of your mailing piece — so that most direct mail packages (such as the ones we spoke of in Chapter 9) will require no more than the minimum postage. As this is written, the third class rate for two and a fraction ounces is 12.5 cents.

That is a mail order owner's bargain — because you can mail a very effective and very elaborate package for that rate.

To mail third class material requires a simple permit — but it must meet rather complicated USPS rules. Most mail order companies have professional mailing houses handle their third class mailing because of the many "breakdowns" required. (That is, first you have to "break down" a third class mailing by ZIP Code, then by two number groups, then three number groups, etc.)

If you use a mailing house, make sure you are provided with a copy of USPS Form 3602, which will establish the date of mailing and the number of pieces which were mailed.

## Using BREs

As we have already noted, virtually all direct mail packages contain a BRE — business reply envelope — to encourage the customer to order quickly — and without having to pay any postage.

As you might expect, the money which is saved by the customer is paid for by the mail order company.

That price might be higher than you anticipated — but we will share with you a method of sharply reducing it.

To include BREs with your mailings, you will need a Business Reply Permit — USPS Form 3614. As this is written, that fee is only $50 per year.

For that annual fee, the post office will deliver all BREs to you — for regular first class postage *plus* a fee of 23¢ per envelope. That is a considerable premium for providing your customers with "postage paid" privileges.

There is, however, an alternative BRE fee arrangement available to mail order companies.

As an alternative, you can pay a $160 annual accounting fee in addition to the $50 fee noted above *and* maintain a constant deposit at the post office to cover the on-going BRE delivery charges. If you agree to these terms, then the delivery fee for each returned BRE is reduced to 7¢!

If you expect to receive more than 518 BREs in one year, then you should select the second option.

## Additional Postal Information

This short chapter is not intended as a postal primer. The USPS has many free documents which it will make available to you, and the U.S. Government Printing Office publishes a wide range of postal data.

You can write to the Superintendent of Documents, U.S. Government Printing Office, Washington, D.C. 20402, for a complete list of USPS-related publications.

# 14

# WHEN TO MAIL — AND WHEN NOT TO MAIL

In life, according to a well-known expression, timing is everything.

In the mail order business, timing *really* is everything!

## When Should You Mail Your DM Packages?

There used to be nearly unanimous agreement among mail order experts that September and January were the best months during which to mail.

By "best" we mean those months when consumers are most likely to respond to mail order offers in the greatest numbers.

September and January are still very effective and profitable direct mail months.

Now, however, the historical concept of "best months" has been expanded to encompass "best periods."

By this new standard, January through March and August through November are considered to be the prime mailing periods.

Every mail order company has its own individual experience, but the "best periods" represent a strong consensus reflective of the mail order industry overall. Most mail order companies would agree that these two periods are, in fact, "the best."

## When Shouldn't You Mail?

There is no similar agreement when it comes to determining the worst periods.

Mail order is a year-round business yet the "best" periods to mail include only seven of a year's twelve months. Does that mean that nothing should be mailed during the other five months?

Obviously not, but these less productive periods demand a much more cautious approach.

Most mail order experts would agree that July and December are months to avoid. They typically result in failed mailings — and very few major mailings are undertaken during these difficult months.

Your mail order business will develop its own track record, but these guidelines are based on the historical performance of many companies over an extended period of time and can safely serve as a basis for your "mailing calendar" until you have created your own response data.

# CHAPTER
# 15

# HOW TO USE THE "OLD" TECHNOLOGIES — AND THE NEW ONES

In a so-called "high-tech" world, where miniature computer chips can hold literally millions of pieces of information, the mail order business remains singularly "low-tech."

Direct mail, catalogues and newspaper and magazine advertising — the three primary categories of the mail order business — do not require much of the sophistication of modern engineering. Certainly, computer technology has improved the ability of each of these categories to more efficiently identify and reach prospects, but fundamentally mail order remains a very "basic" business.

As we mentioned in Chapter 1, these three categories will remain the foundation of the mail order business for years to come. However, they are no longer a mail order business' *exclusive* means of communicating with its audience.

Today, mail order advertisers have a broad new spectrum of marketing media available to them. More and more advertisers are at least beginning to test them. Only time and experience will determine whether they will be as profitable and effective as the traditional media — but every mail order business owner in the '80's must become familiar with them.

## The "Old" Technologies: Radio and "Regular" Television

Radio and non-cable television have been available as advertising media for mail order businesses for many years.

Very few mail order advertisers use traditional network television, primarily because of its enormous cost. A small group of powerful mail order advertisers do use network television. Typically, they will use it in support of a traditional mail order campaign, to induce viewers to look for their package when it arrives in the mail. The most prominent users of this type of support advertising are the two major national magazine subscription companies.

Smaller mail order companies have occasionally advertised on local television stations, usually late at night when the rates are lower, and some of them have succeeded with this approach. Nevertheless, non-cable TV is not a scheduled component in most mail order advertising campaigns.

Radio has been employed with somewhat greater frequency — for several reasons. It is relatively inexpensive and it can be ordered on very short notice. For some advertisers, radio has worked well; for others, it has not. Years ago, when leading radio stations employed "personalities," mail order success was greater than it is today because the personality's reading of the commercial was considered to be equivalent to a personal endorsement by his faithful listeners.

Thus, on balance, the level of mail order advertising on both radio and non-cable television has essentially remained very modest over the years.

## The Birth of
## The "New" Technologies

More recently, four new media categories have become available — and all of them, to one degree or another, are being used and tested by some mail order advertisers.

These four categories are: 1. Cable television; 2. Home video; 3. Computers, and 4. Telemarketing.

We shall consider each of them.

### 1. Cable Television

Cable television has been compared to special-category magazines.

If a mail order advertiser wanted to reach fisherman, say, he could confidently place his ad in *Field & Stream*. Similarly, if his target audience was financial executives, he could safely place his ad in *Forbes*.

Cable television has similar qualities, as so-called "narrowcasting" channels have been created.

Additionally, cable television — unlike traditional network television — will accept commercials which are longer than the standard 30 or 60-second network commercials. Most mail order marketing experts believe that an effective mail order TV commercial must be at least 90 seconds long, and preferably 120 seconds.

Thus, an advertiser selling a guidebook to Europe can buy time on *The Travel Channel* and the advertiser who used *Field & Stream* in our above example can use ESPN, the all-sports cable network. And, not to forget our *Forbes* advertiser, he can now reach his desired prospects on FNN — the Financial News Network.

In addition to the special-interest cable networks, cable

"superstations," like Ted Turner's WTBS, are also available. They have many characteristics similar to the traditional networks — ABC, CBS and NBC — in that they reach a wide, national audience, but they also have the advantage of flexibility, of accommodating the marketing needs of mail order advertisers. WTBS, in fact, has single-handedly established the success of a wide variety of mail order products.

It is too early to tell how the cable networks will develop, but, as this is being written, there is no question but that they have enhanced the available marketing options for many mail order advertisers.

We should add a postscript about the most recent cable television innovation, the so-called "home shopping networks." Their entire business consists of mail order advertising! They have done well in their early stages, but questions remain about their long-term effectiveness. In any event, they represent a very interesting development — and confirm the ability of cable television to sell mail order merchandise.

## 2. Home Video

At first, the home video business (the sales and rental of tapes for use by viewers at home) consisted primarily of motion pictures, how-to tapes (most prominently, Jane Fonda's famous "workout" tape) and children's programming.

More recently, advertisers have entered the home video market — by "sponsoring" programs available on tape. Presumably, their participation in the production of the program lowered the cost for home video users, who (theoretically) didn't mind that the tradeoff for this savings was some exposure to the sponsor's message. To date, these sponsored tapes have achieved moderate success — but they are still few in number, and most advertisers are cautiously exploring this new technique. While this home video category appears certain to expand, it will apparently do so at a very moderate pace.

The newest home video dimension has been the introduction of "home video catalogues" and "home video magazines." The "catalogues" are similar to the home shopping cable TV approach, and the "magazines" carry commercials within them. Both are too new to evaluate with any confidence.

## 3. Computers

A number of computer networks have been created, enabling owners of home (and office) computers to "link up" with the services and data which they provide. Several of them offer their subscribers the ability to order merchandise through this link-up.

None of these computer networks have sufficient subscribers or sufficient marketing data to make an informed judgment with respect to their value to mail order advertisers.

Some observers, however, believe that computers have attractive long-term prospects for mail order advertisers.

## 4. Telemarketing

800 numbers are telemarketing's answer to the BRE — a technique encouraging consumers to respond to mail order offers without any expense.

And so-called WATS lines (Wide Area Telephone Service) are telemarketing's equivalent to bulk mailings — enabling advertisers to reach prospects at sharply reduced quantity rates.

"Telemarketing" is really a fancy expression for the use of telephones by mail order advertisers to reach prospects — and for consumers to reach these advertisers in return.

No matter how you describe it, telemarketing has many beneficial applications for mail order advertisers — and telemarketing will grow as an increasingly important mail order advertising technique.


The beginning mail order entrepreneur will most likely not employ any of these technologies (old or new) in the start-up phase of his mail order business. In time, however, he will probably begin to use some or all of them — and, by that time, there will probably be new ones that haven't even been invented as this book goes to press!

# 16

# THE IMPORTANCE OF ACCURATE, USEFUL RECORD-KEEPING

It is important for every business to maintain accurate records; it is especially important for mail order businesses to do so.

Your accountant's advice, your lawyer's recommendations, and the particular needs of your specific business operation will determine your precise record-keeping requirements. We will, however, touch on some of the records which must generally be established and maintained by *all* mail order businesses.

## Customer Records

You will recall our lengthy discussion in Chapter 3 about the FTC's "30 Day Rule." The "clock" begins to run on the day you receive the customer's completed order; therefore, you must maintain very accurate records with respect to the receipt of orders.

There are many other reasons, as well, for maintaining

very complete and very current customer records.

They will enable you to answer any questions from customers, should they arise. And, from a marketing perspective, the more information which you have about a customer (what he ordered, when he ordered it, when he re-ordered, etc.), the more valuable he becomes to you in terms of being able to target him for specific advertising campaigns.

## Advertising Expenses

You not only have to keep track of how much money you spent on each aspect of your advertising, you have to match that data with the results of each aspect of your advertising.

There are many ways to accomplish this — both manually and by computer — and you will have to have a system in place which works for you. Your accountant and/or a computer consultant can help you set up a system which will provide the information you need.

## Inventory Expenses

Merchandise sitting on your shelf, waiting to be ordered and delivered, is an expense.

It is difficult at the very beginning to know how much stock you should maintain in order to fill orders promptly — without having excess inventory which costs you money for so long as it isn't sold.

It is important to be able to make such a judgment as quickly and accurately as possible, and the sooner you have a reliable formula, the better off you will be.

## "Hidden" Expenses in The Mail Order Business

You will have to make some provisions for certain expenses which are uniquely applicable to the mail order business. Some of these include:

*Credit card discount:* If your customer ordered a $10 item but paid for it by a credit card which charges you 4%, you did not really receive $10. Your real income on this order was $9.60 — $10 less 40¢ (4%).

*Reserve for returns:* A certain percentage of customers (typically very small) will return the merchandise which they ordered. You will have to make an accounting provision for the sum total of such anticipated returns.

*Lost shipments:* Some shipments will get lost in transit, and you will have to re-ship them at your expense. You may or may not be covered by insurance for these losses. In any event, you will have to make provisions for them in your record-keeping of projected profit and loss.

*Bounced checks:* Sometimes, even after waiting before sending an order paid for by personal check, that check will be returned to you because of "insufficient finds." The bank will charge you a fee for returning that uncollected check — and you will have additional expenses if you attempt to collect the money due from your customer who is in arrears.

*Uncollected sales tax:* Say a customer in your own state fails to add the appropriate sales tax to his payment. You will in all likelihood elect to accept his order and pay the difference rather than reject the order or attempt to collect the tax. That is an expense which you must consider — and record.

These are simply some examples of expenses which can easily be "forgotten." A mail order business, which often operates on close profit-and-loss margins, cannot afford to "forget" any expenses.

The IRS expects you to maintain accurate and complete records; the FTC and the Post Office expect you to maintain accurate records, and your customers expect you to maintain accurate records.

Most importantly, however, you must expect yourself to maintain complete and accurate records. They are the "barometer" of your business — and you must be able to determine the condition of your business 24 hours a day, 365 days a year.

CHAPTER

# 17

# 10 EASY-TO-START MAIL ORDER START-UP OPPORTUNITIES

You are welcome to take any of these 10 mail order product ideas and make them your own.

That, however, is not the true purpose of this chapter.

This chapter is really designed to provide you with a sense of the *unlimited* opportunities which are available to the mail order entrepreneur!

From time to time throughout this book, we have mentioned that one of the most exciting aspects of the mail order business is that it can be started *anywhere at any time!* To that, we will now add — *with anything!*

Who would have ever believed that someone could come up with the idea of a "pet rock" — and turn that idea into millions of dollars?

The most unlikely products have turned entrepreneurs into mail order millionaires — and some of the "surest things" have failed. There is no guaranteed formula for mail order success. *Rather, it is a combination of traditional business skills coupled with the desire to create and market exciting and useful products to a world filled with people willing to give anyone the opportunity to succeed!*

We hope that you will find these 10 ideas interesting and useful — and that they will inspire you to come up with 10 better ideas of your own!

We gave ourselves a personal challenge before sitting down to write this next-to-last chapter: To come up with these 10 ideas in 10 minutes. One mail order idea a minute!

*Imagine what you can do with all the time in the world!*

### 1. A Recipe Booklet

Self-publishing is one of the easiest entries in the world of mail order. Think of 50 of your favorite recipes — ones you've improved on with your own skill and imagination — and put them together in a small booklet.

### 2. Senior Citizen Newsletter

Maybe you are one (a "senior citizen") or you have close friends or relatives in that category. Put together the most useful, helpful tips you can think of for this audience — and create a monthly newsletter for the 60-plus market.

### 3. Needlepoint Kits of People's Homes

Invite people to send you photographs or sketches of their homes — which you will convert into a needlepoint pattern for them to knit. Consumers love to order personalized items. What's more personal than a needlepoint rendering of their own home?

### 4. Cassette Telephone Messages

Come up with six clever messages for telephone answering machines — and record them on a cassette. Offer that cassette for sale with some entertaining copy and see what kind of response you get. Millions of people have answering machines — and most of them hate recording their own messages!

## 5. A Personalized Product
Mail order's most successful woman — Lillian Vernon — has built a mail order empire on the premise that consumers love to see their name or initials on products. Create a personalized product which takes advantage of this successful and profitable premise.

## 6. Labels For Clothes
Millions of people make their own clothes. Create personalized labels for them to attach to their handiwork. "Jane Doe" will take greater pride in a "Made in the Studio of Jane Doe" label than in one from Macy's or Bloomingdale's!

## 7. A Fad
Try to come up with a fad. Just remember, "pet rocks" have already been done!

## 8. Square Dance Instruction
You've been square dancing since your first church social — and you can still move with the best of callers! Create a videotape or an audiocassette or simply a booklet of your own special square dance techniques.

## 9. 50 Things To Do With Your 2-Year-Old This Weekend
You may be a "Yuppie" or a grandfather. In either case, you have the expertise to put together this helpful and entertaining "instruction" booklet.

## 10. A Tool You've Invented
You've solved more problems around the house with a

funny-looking gadget you've been using for years. Check it out. What's helped you might be equally useful for millions of other do-it- yourselfers!

*Now, it's your turn!*

# 18

# MAIL ORDER AND YOU

*Mail order and you.*

We hope that you like the sound of that sentence — that it feels "good" and "right" for you.

Perhaps you started reading this book simply to find out a little more about the mail order business.

Hopefully, what you've read has provided you with an encouraging (and realistic) sense of the many opportunities which the mail order business holds.

The mail order business offers the promise of greater excitement and self-fulfillment than many businesses. It also contains many risks.

You'll never be certain about the success of a particular product or offer until your mailbox tells you. If it's empty, you'll feel about the same. If it's crammed with envelopes filled with orders — *and money* — you'll feel like you've won the lottery!

The mail order business is not an appropriate enterprise for everyone.

If it is a suitable and comfortable business for you, we hope that the end of this book is a new beginning for you: As a mail order entrepreneur!

# SELECTED MAIL ORDER WORDS AND PHRASES

**Active Customer:** Any mail order buyer who has ordered within the past year.

**Address Correction Requested (ACR):** An instruction to the Postal Service usually printed in the upper left-hand corner of an outside envelope. For a fee (currently 30¢), the USPS will advise you of the addressee's forwarding address. ACR is usually used to "clean" a mailing list, to keep it current and accurate.

**Back-end:** This expression has two small order meanings. 1. It simply means the fulfillment of an order. 2. It represents what a customer has ordered beyond his initial purchase. Therefore, a strong "back-end" can be a double blessing for a mail order business: It can signify efficient fulfillment operations and profitable customers who engage in high-margin repeat business.

**Bounce-back:** An offer added to a fulfilled order, encouraging the buyer to make an additional purchase upon receipt of his order.

**Bulk Mail:** Third class mail, the most frequently used category of mail delivery service employed by mail order businesses.

**Business Reply Envelope (BRE):** An envelope provided to prospective mail order customers enabling them to mail their orders without having to pay postage. Postage (plus a fee to the post office) is paid by the addressee, the mail order company.

**Coding:** A system, usually combining letters and numbers, enabling a mail order advertiser to determine the particular advertisement or mailing which produced his orders.

**Co-op Mailing:** A mailing shared by two or more mail order advertisers, with each paying their share of the promotion.

**Cost Per Inquiry:** A formula to determine the cost of each inquiry received. One divides the cost of the advertisement or mailing by the number of inquiries.

**Cost Per Order:** The same formula as above as applied to the actual number of orders.

**Decoy (or Dummy) Names:** Names added to a mailing list by the owner to ascertain that a list user is not using his list other than the list rental agreement permits.

**Direct Marketing:** An expanded definition of mail order, which uses three traditional marketing methods — direct mail, catalogues and newspapers and magazines — to solicit business. Direct marketing includes mail order as well as conventional television, radio, cable television, home video, computer data bases, and telemarketing.

**800 Number:** A toll-free telephone number provided to mail order purchasers, enabling them to place an order at no charge.

**Mailing List Broker:** An organization or an individual which manages mailing lists for owners and rents them to users.

**Offer:** The terms of the sales agreement between mail order advertisers and mail order buyers. An offer must contain the price and the terms of purchase (cash or credit, extended payments, etc.). Virtually all mail order offers include a guarantee (a pledge of customer satisfaction), as well.

**Package:** The components of an offer to prospective mail order buyers, most often transmitted by mail. A package usually consists of five parts: The outside envelope, a sales letter, a sales brochure, an order form and a return envelope.

**Response Rate:** The percentage of inquiries or orders received from a particular advertisement or mailing. For example, if a mailing of 1000 pieces produced 25 inquiries or orders, the response rate would be two-and-one-half percent (2.5%).

**Standard Industrial Classification (S.I.C.):** A classification of companies by category, as developed by the U.S. Department of Commerce. "Business-to-business" mailing lists are often available by S.I.C.

**ZIP Code:** The United States Postal Service's system of digits designed to expedite the delivery of mail. Originally, a system based on five digits, it is being expanded to nine digits for greater speed and accuracy.

# SOURCES OF ADDITIONAL INFORMATION

**Department of Commerce, 14th Street and Constitution Avenue, NW, Washington, DC 20230, (202) 377-2000.** For information on how to market your products around the world and for data regarding foreign companies seeking American marketing and distribution.

**Directory of Conventions, 1518 Walnut Street, Philadelphia, PA 19102, (215) 546-3295.** An annual directory listing every major (and minor) trade show in the United States.

**Direct Mail List Rates & Data, 3004 Glenview Road, Wilmette, IL 60091, (312) 256-6067.** The title is an accurate description of its contents. The media "bible" of the mail order business.

**Direct Marketing Association, Inc., 6 East 43rd Street, New York, NY 10017, (212) 689-4977.** A very active and useful mail order business trade association which will send you a "Membership Information Kit" upon request.

**Federal Trade Commission, Pennsylvania Avenue at 6th Street, NW, Washington, DC 20580, (202) 523-3830.** For a copy of the FTC 30-Day Rule and other information with respect to the FTC's jurisdiction over interstate mail order sales.

**Thomas' Register of American Manufacturers, One Penn Plaza, New York, NY 10001, (212) 290-7262.** Again, the title describes its contents. The telephone number provided is Thomas' Information Service number which will assist you in locating companies of interest to you.

**U.S. Postal Service, 475 L'Enfant Plaza SW, Washington, DC 20260, (202) 268-2000.** For all general and specific postal information. However, your local post office should be your first source of inquiry.

# ABOUT THE AUTHOR

Steve Kahn is an attorney and entrepreneur. As an entrepreneur, he has created new businesses in publishing, cable television and real estate. He has been the Executive Producer of "The Miss American Teen-Ager Pageant" for the ABC Television Network and a feature columnist for The New York Times Syndicate with a weekly audience of ten million Sunday newspaper readers. As an attorney, he served as Special Counsel and Director of Investor Relations for the Tishman Real Estate & Construction Co., Inc. He holds a B.S. degree from New York University and a J.D. degree from New York Law School.

# ABOUT THE NO NONSENSE
# SUCCESS SERIES

More people than ever before are thinking about going into business for themselves — and the No Nonsense Success Guides have been created to provide useful information for this growing and ambitious audience. Look for these related No Nonsense Success Guides: *The Self-Employment Test . . . How To Run A Business Out Of Your Home . . . How To Own And Operate A Franchise . . . How (and Where) To Get The Money To Get Started . . . Getting Into The Consulting Business.*